From Sheep
to Scarf

From Sheep
to Scarf

Ali Mitgutsch

 Carolrhoda Books, Inc., Minneapolis

First published in the United States of America 1981 by
Carolrhoda Books, Inc. All English language rights reserved.

Original edition © 1971 by Sellier Verlag GmbH, Eching bei München,
West Germany, under the title VOM SCHAF ZUM SCHAL.
Revised English text © 1981 by Carolrhoda Books, Inc.
Illustrations © 1971 by Sellier Verlag GmbH.

Manufactured in the United States of America

LIBRARY OF CONGRESS CATALOGING IN PUBLICATION DATA

Mitgutsch, Ali.
  From sheep to scarf.

    (A Carolrhoda start to finish book)
    First published under title: Vom Schaf Zum Schal.
    SUMMARY: Highlights the step-by-step process of
  shearing sheep, spinning wool, and knitting a scarf.

    1. Woolen and worsted manufacture—Juvenile litera-
  ture. [1. Wool] I. Title.

  TS1626.M5713   1981   677′.31   80-29557
  ISBN 0-87614-164-5

        1 2 3 4 5 6 7 8 9 10 86 85 84 83 82 81

From Sheep to Scarf

Here is a shepherd watching over his sheep.
Every day he takes them to a meadow
so that they can eat grass.
His sheep dog helps him.

The sheep grow thick woolen coats.

Every spring the shepherd cuts them off.

This is called **shearing**.

The sheep will grow new coats over the summer
to keep them warm next winter.

After the shepherd has sheared his sheep,
he puts the wool into bales.
The bales are loaded onto a truck
and taken to a factory.
The factory is called a **spinning mill**.

At the spinning mill the wool is spun into yarn.

Today this is done by large machines.

But long ago it was done by hand
with spinning wheels.

First a machine combs and untangles the wool.

Then it twists the wool into long strands of yarn.

The yarn is still the color of sheep's wool.
Most of it is white or the color of cream.
But some of it may be gray or black.
The light-colored yarn can be dyed
many different colors.

Now the yarn is ready to go to stores
where it will be sold.
Emily is buying some yarn for her grandmother.

Grandmother is knitting a red scarf.

She uses two long, straight knitting needles.

The ball of yarn is still big

and the scarf is already long!

What else can Grandmother make

from the red yarn?

Now Emily has a hat, a scarf, mittens,
and socks all made from red yarn.
All of this beautiful wool came from sheep.
And it will keep Emily warm all winter long!

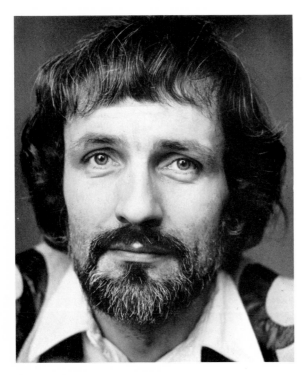

Ali
Mitgutsch

ALI MITGUTSCH is one of Germany's best-known children's book illustrators. He is a devoted world traveler, and many of his book ideas have taken shape during his travels. Perhaps this is why they have such international appeal. Mr. Mitgutsch's books have been published in 22 countries and are enjoyed by thousands of readers around the world.

Ali Mitgutsch lives with his wife and three children in Schwabing, the artists' quarter in Munich. The Mitgutsch family also enjoys spending time on their farm in the Bavarian countryside.

# THE CAROLRHODA
>>> START

From Beet to Sugar

From Blossom to Honey

From Cacao Bean to Chocolate

From Cement to Bridge

From Clay to Bricks

From Cotton to Pants

From Cow to Shoe

From Dinosaurs to Fossils

From Egg to Bird

From Egg to Butterfly

From Fruit to Jam

From Grain to Bread

From Grass to Butter

From Ice to Rain

From Milk to Ice Cream

From Oil to Gasoline

From Ore to Spoon

From Sand to Glass

From Seed to Pear

From Sheep to Scarf

From Tree to Table

TO FINISH >>>
BOOKS